The Ups and Downs

of being in your 60s

INTRODUCTION

There's no reason to approach your 60s with trepidation. It's a wonderful age to be. Think about it: there's very little left for you to learn the hard way; when you throw a party, the neighbours aren't going to complain; you'll always be younger than Mick Jagger!

Once you hit your stride, you'll stop worrying about all those little things like your mortgage, your career, your reputation and all that other stuff you can't seem to remember any more. Be the person you always secretly dreamed of being and wear Hawaiian shirts to the shops, take long naps in the afternoon, and hum loudly along to the muzak in the lift. You won't give a damn if anybody notices.

By this stage of course, the body is one thing; the mind's another. The former may be telling you to slow down, but if you train it properly your brain will be telling you to take everything to the limit. Better to burn out than to fade away, well that's what Neil Young said anyway.

So go on adventure holidays, take up sky-diving, buy a big crazy hat, learn Finnish, skip down the street, or get yourself an allotment and hoist the Jolly Roger above it. The world is your oyster when you have a free bus pass. Life begins at 60.

Tony Husband

'OK! Do we take the sensible route or the more demanding one?'

'It's my bucket list.'

'Robert! Who advised you to buy those jeans?!!'

'Jane, wake up. I've turned 60!'

'Barry, have you been tampering with this mirror?'

'Yay... free bus pass.'

'Why are you always Batman when we go to fancy dress parties?'

'I hope you won't take offence, Tim, but you have the underpants drawer of a much younger man.'

'... age 60s, she must be into trainspotting.'

'He's showing his age again.'

'Can I read the number plate on what car?'

'I'm retiring soon, Max. I need someone to take my place.'

'Tom, don't you think it's time you started wearing pyjamas in bed?'

'Darling, I forget... do two or three of our children go to university?'

'Well, to be honest, Ralph, I see no sense in taking up devil worship in your 60s.'

'It's bad news, Sis, he got the all-clear.'

'Aren't you coming to bed? It's nearly 10 o'clock.'

'I often dream of flying off to exotic locations. Strangely, Ben, you're never with me.'

'Not a single pair of matching socks... why?'

'Hi, Jan, open the wine. My kidney function tests were clear.'

'Dad, can you turn your music down?'

'Yes, she does look amazing for her age. So would I if I was married to a plastic surgeon.'

'Will you all stop singing "The Final Countdown"?'

'Scuse me, where can I find the fountain of youth?'

'There's Jack. He avoids the first 18 holes and starts at the 19th these days.'

'We were just laughing at you in these photos of your wedding...
your hairstyle!!'

'I'll be the one to tell you whether I'm a control freak or not, Denise.'

'My husband's a rambler... not that he goes walking, he just talks far too much.'

'Thinking about it, I'm only 10 in dog years.'

'There they are! Oh no, T-shirt clash.'

'Did the doctor prescribe that double-scoop ice cream to go with your statins, Lawrence?'

'The satnav says bear right, but I haven't seen a single one...'

'One of my regrets, Deirdre, is that the Swinging Sixties never swung for me.'

'Grandad, Grandma's just shown me this photo of you when you were younger.'

'I wonder if Mick Jagger uses his bus pass.'

'Him? Huh, all he does is stare at the fish.'

'Stop that, George, every time Mother calls round.'

'Wig?!! How did you know I'm wearing one?'

'I remember first hearing that Beatles song and thinking,
"No fear of ever being that old".'

'You're going to have to strap yourself in, John,
if you want to try out my new home brew.'

'I'm so glad you're here, babe. This gentleman in his 60s has been chatting me up.'

'Oh dear, Geoffrey, you've gone back 400 years now and they're all as boring as you.'

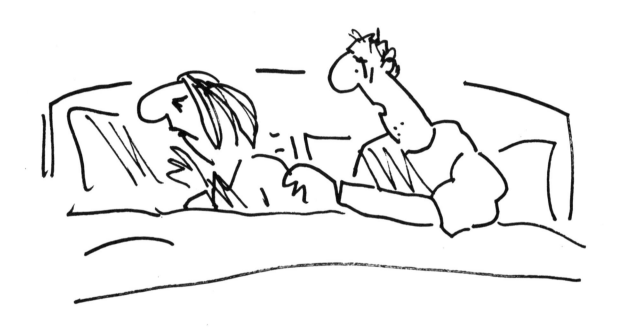

'Glynnis, wake up... tell me I'm not 60 today.' 'You're not, Malcolm, you're 61.'

'Off to a rock concert?! At your age, you should be going to your allotment.'

'Ambulance please... Hello, it's my husband. He's spontaneously combusted.'

'We're hoping you prefer older men.'

'Do you remember when we'd sit here talking about the good old days?'

'For heaven's sake, you've retired, Peter... Relax!'

'It's a belated retirement present, dear, basically to get you out of the house and out from under my feet.'

'Besides bed blocking, what are your main worries about being in your 60s?'

'Neil Young said it all: "Better to burn out than to fade away."
Another half, Walter?'

'It's our 40th anniversary next month... what comes after Silver and Pearl, is it Cement?'

'Oh no, I've moved into the cardigans–every–birthday age.'

'I'm divorcing my husband. He's a ventriloquist and snores on my side of the bed.'

'I keep getting emails about planning my funeral.'

'What have you done with my Speedos?!'

'George, do we always need to have a nanny on standby just in case the grandchildren come round?'

'Life's never been dull. We once had a library book that was overdue for several days...'

'Why don't you go into the garden and curse the mole hills? That always cheers you up.'

'Retirement's becoming like a stray dog. As soon as you approach it, it runs away.'

'I'd rather have grey hair in my 60s than no hair in my 40s.'

'Yes, Rob, I know it's a rescue donkey and you felt sorry for it, but I ask again where are we going to keep it?'

'Can you call back, he's trying to out-stare the dog?'

'Apparently, my dad's new girlfriend is younger than us.'

'You love me. I can't believe it! Is that you talking or is it the beer?'
'Er, it's me talking to the beer.'

'Hi, Mandy, it's Clare. We were trying to remember if your
Alex is still alive.'

'Used to be a hare, now I'm more of a tortoise.'

'To be honest, dear, since you turned 60 your bum looks big in anything.'

'Oh, *wowie zowie*, Mrs Barton, now I know where Nuala gets her stunning looks!'

'£4.90 for a beer?! My first pint cost me 1s 6d.'

'I'm guessing plastic surgery.'

'Buy him a pint and he'll tell you all about seeing the Beatles and the Stones in little bars and pubs in the 60s.'

'Strange how he becomes my dog when he's done something wrong.'

'Is there something wrong between us, Rupert?'

'Darling, shouldn't you get your ears tested?' 'Beers... yes, I'll have one thanks.'

'(Gasp). Inside, I'm still every bit the athlete I always was, Julie.'

'While you're in there, ask them if they can find out if you've got a heart.'

'You said you'd teach me how to surf the net, son.'

'You want to see your future... are you sure?'

'Guinness Book of Records? Hi, what's the highest blood pressure reading ever?'

'Isn't it about time you got a sensible car?'

'I still like going to gigs but only if I can sit down.'

'This wine is rather like myself: maturing beautifully.'

'What do we have here? Oh yes, a 60-year-old boy racer!'

'It's lovely and there's so much scope for a granny flat.'

'Special delivery for you, luv.'

'Mum, Dad, I don't love my husband any more. I want to move back here.' 'Don't you love him a little bit?'

'Free prescriptions, free transport, free eye tests equals more wine for us.'

'Sixty years old, Harry... but in my mind I'm 21.'

'Oh no, he's on his flipping trampoline again.'

'Yes, your new trousers are very nice, dear, perhaps a tad high in the waistband.'

'Hi, Michael won't be coming. He can't stand you.'

'You... you... you're stopping my pocket money?! Just wait till I tell Grandad about this!'

'Dancing on tables at your age!'

'Mum, Dad... holidays?! Who's going to look after the children?'

'We're slowly drifting apart, aren't we, Ralph?'

'Can you keep your voice down? I don't want everyone to hear.'

'(Sigh) It's taking longer and longer to scroll back to the year of my birth.'

'Yes, pal, I may be old, but at least I own my home and car, take three holidays a year, and have a very substantial pension.'

'Don't leave me, Tracy, how will I survive?'

'Psst, Bernie, what's my wife's name again? I've got to introduce her to someone.'

'So, Mr Booth, you're looking for a lady in her mid-30s and you're, erm, 67. I think *we* should start getting real here.'

'Your father was a pub philosopher, son. He contemplated the
meaning of beer for many years....'

'We've just bought a second home. It's nice and out of the way.'

'Janice, I just remembered my old vinyl collection. This is going to be so much fun.'

'I bought her from a man in the pub. We'll be self-sufficient in no time... (hic)'

'Just because I receive a pension doesn't mean I'm a pensioner.'

'Tch, the weather report said cloudless skies!!'

'I wish my wife would leave me for a younger man.'

'Did we really drink all the wine last night?'

'I'm younger than Mick Jagger, you know.'

'This satnav's for people in their 60s. It's very loud and speaks much too slowly and clearly.'

'The doctor's given me a shopping list: new hearing aid, new hip, new knee.'

'I'm warning all the single males that Nancy's just got here and she's on the hunt for a new husband.'

'We had our little grand-daughter stopping over the weekend.'

'Lads, the drinks are on me. My wife has lost her voice.'

'On that money, you'd think they might win occasionally.'

'My looks are fading, Eric.' 'Well, at least your eyesight's still working.'

'Oh, that's just my husband practising for when he's an angel.'

'Stop whingeing. Wait until you're in your 70s!'